TO: ME, FROM: ME.

DARSANA RAVINDRAN

Made with ♥ on the Notion Press Platform
www.notionpress.com

To,

Everyone, because the people pleaser in me worries about how someone would feel if they're names weren't mentioned.

The title says it's to yourself, what's that about then?

Honestly who cares?

Me! My mind! It won't stop pestering me about it.

Okay I should stop having this one way conversation before I creep my readers out even more.

Let's try this again shall we?

To,

Amma, Acha, Dhadha, Bhabi, Nene, Ana, Appucha, Keeki, Teeku, Cutay, Smimi, T-Rex, Manish, Partner, Little one and Everyone who's taken the time to read my book.

The nicknames are wild, I know.

Thank you for always believing in me and reminding me that I am capable of more everyday.

I love you guys.

Contents

Contents

Preface

As I type this down, it's the first time I've ever felt blank when writing, there is no train of thoughts, possibly because the reality of finally publishing this book has weighed down on me. But even then, let me try my best to give the most plausible description that's close to showing what's in store for you with this book.

Words have always been a freeing path of escape for my unattended emotions and so through this book I hope to remind myself and tell everybody small parts of my story. I like to think that my poems are little snippets, maybe a trailer representing the way my mind works. There's both the good and the bad days and I have taken them as they've come, documenting them in my own creative ways.

I realized that the words I put on my phone screen could be put on a cream sheet of paper and here we are today in hopes that this book encourages everyone to write down their thoughts and share them with the world while they're at it, for you never know which small piece could be the biggest realisation and maybe even a savior to someone and maybe even yourself.

With no much more to say, I am going to let you experience the roller coaster of thoughts that capture the mind I like to call mine.

Darsana.

Acknowledgements

Mimi? Ravttacha?

I did it!

I finally put my first book out!

Are you proud of me? Please tell me you are, because that validation just might make my inner child feel a little better.

Putting all that aside, Thankyou from the bottom of my legs, because from the heart would be a little too less of space, for always encouraging me to write more. Thankyou for the hundred books you've bought me to write on, even though most of them have only their first 19 pages filled. Why 19? I don't know, it's just a rough figure.

Dhadha, Etta, my ride or die,

Thank you.

No amount of words would ever give meaning to the gratitude I have for solely your existence and even more for your support. You've always helped me do better and be better. Letting me explore and live to myself is a decision you took and supported me through, I'll always remember and thank you a million times for that.

Bhabi,

It's only been a while but Thank You for taking me as your own. Your cheers always stay special and I couldn't be more grateful to call you family. Your smile makes me believe that I do a great job and that I can grow better.

Nene, hubby, twin,

I have too much to thank you for. When I stay low you make sure you push me up and high, when I ignore, you make me listen and accept. Thankyou for everything you've done and are doing. It's always easier when you're around and I know you've got my back always. Thank you for letting me be weird around you. Let's always work together to get better at this living life thing.

To the people that got me through high school and continues to get me through life,

Ana, Appucha, keeki,

I love you and thank you.

You've seen me struggle through some of the hardest years of my life and gave me nothing but support and love.

You guys make me feel the luckiest everyday.

You made me feel special, when I felt ordinary,

made me see power, when I saw weakness,

made me see light, when I saw darkness.

Thank you.

Smimi,

Thankyou for taking care of me, Thankyou for protecting me, Thankyou for surviving with me, Thankyou for being you with me, Thankyou for letting me be myself with you. What you were, what you are, what you will be remains special to me.

Teeku, Cutay

Thankyou for being my girls. Finding you both was possibly, no, definitely the best thing that happened to me during those three years. Everything I did, you looked at me with pride and your support and love is always appreciated. I can't thank you enough for staying for not just the good but the worst as well. You will always be my girls.

Partner, Manish,

Thankyou for being the ones I could run to at any hour of the day. Every conversation with the both of you stays recorded in my mind and is something I'd always cherish. Everytime I doubted myself, all I had to think about was what you both would tell me and I know I can get through it just fine.

T-Rex,

Girl you really vibed with me at a different level and I love it always. You were that person who understood what it meant to leave home and be in a new place and you helped me get through that just fine. Thankyou for always cracking some great jokes and always making me laugh. I'm starting to believe that I actually might be in love with you.

Little one,

It'll never hit me that you've grown up, but everytime you help me through things, I know you'll do just fine. But this is not about that, this is about how grateful I am for having you. This is about how grateful I am that we connect through dance. This is about how grateful I am for having someone to rant to and to never be judged because you'd do the same.

Thankyou to each and every one of you.

1. Being Human

The need to be loud, to scream what I think remains strong,
Because what if I wasn't loud enough, would I be done wrong?
Tell me I'm right,
Tell me I matter,
Don't gaslight,
Don't let me shatter.
My ego needs validation,
Constant appreciation,
And maybe that is the foundation,
To one of gods weirdest creation.

2. Canvas

My body, a tattered canvas,
Cuts and slashes sliding across,
Red, yellow, blue, all shades,
Smeared fingerprints of invasive hands,
Imprinted insecurities of the wounded,
It's all a scatter,
A canvas nonetheless,
Listen to me as I say,
To me this just may be the most beautiful painting.

3. Even then she shall rise

They moved around her with grins that screamed resemblance to
deceitful faces,
Stuck to her like leeches, sucked all of what she gave so selflessly,
The vultures and hyenas that lick the carcass clean, seemed better
than they who fed on her wounds,
Her silent screams of pain became the fuel they needed to run
their vehicle of greed and power,
They craved her sanity in their own destructive world of insanity,
They leached upon her alluring insanity to cure their own thirst
of success and love,
Yet they lost, stood in front of them was with all the elegance and
grace, HER,
For she knew, jealousy and fear clouded their mind as they
witnessed her flawlessly pick up her broken pieces and fix them
back.

4. Hiraeth

You told me that there's no place like home.
Where's home?
Is it where I have all needs met?
Is it where I keep my struggles?
Is it where my safe space is?
Is it where I feel most threatened?
Is it where I laugh the most?
Is it where I hide and cry?
Is it where I breathe effortlessly?
Is it where I struggle for breath?
Is it where I jump in joy and enjoy?
Is it where I meltdown and stay in lockdown?
Is it where everyone I've always loved stays?
Is it where everyone I've learnt to love stays?
Is it where my family is?
Is it where my friends are?
Is it me?
Am I home?
With all that is entangled in me, am I still capable of being
home?
Is there really no place like mine?

5. My Sweet Child

Household chores went by,
Physically obeying moms orders,
Mentally wanting to be with you.
News came,
You were here ,
The want to impress you fills me,
None of the clothes seem to satisfy me.
Peeking out of the piled up frustration,
Blue,
Your favorite colour,
The color I wore when you first met me.
Would you prefer the jhumkas or the hoops ?
Would you prefer necklace or no necklace ?
Would you prefer red or pink on my lips ?
Should I leave my hair up or free like how I feel when I see you
smile ?
Stupid me.
Stupid me seemed to have forgotten that none of it mattered to
you,
Stupid me seemed to have forgotten that you had seen the real
me,

Stupid me seemed to have forgotten that you loved me in my
plain old pyjamas.
I rushed out to see you being held in my mother's arms,
Dad stood in the corner smiling trying to hide his tears,
Many reminded me what people may think,
Many reminded me that things were to change,
Many reminded me that you weren't mine,
But blood wasn't always the thing that made family right ?
Welcome to your new and forever home my sweet child.

6. Infatuated

A month ago my breathe reeked of alcohol,
A month later I leaked the bottles out,
Curled are my toes,
As you wipe away all my woes,
Your touches, electrifying,
My reaction, terrifying,
You became the strength in my darkness,
And the beauty of my light,
The sweet melody of your whispers,
They quiet down my whimpers,
My previously dull walls seem brighter,
My heart feels lighter,
Your absence makes me whine,
Your presence, smile,
Your mouth pressed against mine,
I feel months pass,
Your head pressed against mine,
I see our love last.

7. The Goddess Within

There she was sitting,
Elegance and grace, with a touch of raw wildness in her posture,
Notice us, hold our gaze they screamed,
She looked,
Swirls of power, courage and strength with a touch of softness in
her eyes,
They craved for her attention,
She stood,
Lifted were the energies and power radiated like a shield,
They begged to be in her presence,
She walked,
The soles of their shoes seem to have melted, for it stayed glued to
where they stood,
They were intimidated by her, she could see their oh so brave
figure breaking,
She smiled,
Shattered was their walls, chaotic was their emotions,
She spoke,
Whatever they thought was the reality of who she was broke into
pieces, scattered, as she stepped on it and left,
She whispered "I hope you know where I stand", looking back,
They nodded, for who was to deny the goddess.

8. Escape the hate and drown in love

It was time to finally find herself,
She opened the door,
Chaos.
How was she to love, when all that was around was hate ?
How was she to accept silence, when all she heard were screams ?
How was she to heal her heart, when the broken pieces showed
no mercy and let her bleed ?
How was she to accept the hand that would let her grow, when
the hand never reached ?
How was she to know what she wanted, where she was headed,
when she had no clue what was in store for her ?
How was she to stop the tears, when she had lost herself ?
How was she to hold on, when nature herself had seem to let go ?
How was she to wake up peacefully, when the nights never
stopped haunting her ?
How was she to be sane, when she found peace in her insanity ?
She closed the door,
For her being wasn't to be exposed to hate but rather drown in
love.

9. Anytime, everytime

And every time it hurts,
Feels like it could kill,
Let me turn it into power,
Let me not take the pill.
And every time it pushes me down,
Scratches all over me,
Let me fix my crown,
Let me fall into something beautiful.

10. What a fool

How foolish was I to think you were ordinary,
When you carried the seed of life itself in you.
How foolish was I to think you weren't watched upon,
When all that surrounds you is synchronization.
How foolish was I to call you wounded,
When your biggest strength was to heal.
How foolish was I to call you weak,
When your tears had the power to flood.
How foolish was I to call you selfish,
When you carried love for everything around.
How foolish I was to ignore you,
When you were everything I should be grateful for.
How foolish of me to think you were a planet,
When you were the universe itself.
Oh, what a fool I was.

11. Remembering you

You were my savior,
You just weren't aware of that failure,
I still remember the first time I saw you,
Khaki coloured pants and the blue shirt never looked that great
on anybody else.
You were everybody's friend,
Just not mine,
When days felt dull,
Just the thought of you and it all seemed so much brighter.
But You were just always running, on the go, hoping, praying to
make it.
And as I remember, I wonder,
Did anyone ask you if you were tired? If all that fame was what
you wanted?
Were you burdened?
Perhaps to keep a name that was stumped upon you.
Today I have no regrets,
Not even of having avoided talking to you,
Where are you, what are you doing, those thoughts never crossed
me anymore,
Until today,
But whatever it is, I hope you're doing okay,

that you still have that smile on you.
I don't feel like I was or am a failure anymore,
But I'm glad I get to call you my savior.

• 13 •

12. Hey you, hey me

Dear body,
I forget,
Forget that you do not know,
Forget that all you know is what I tell you,
What I make you believe,
What I make a habit for you.
So today as I speak to you,
Though we have failed multiple times at this,
Though we are still foreign to this,
Let me speak to you with love,
Let me speak to you with care,
Let me speak to you with softness,
Let me speak to you the way I do to the ones I love,
Let me be with you,
Tell you I'm sorry,
Tell you I accept,
Tell you I love you.

13. Spots on white

Irritation courses through them as your little blots of ink reaches
them,
But not for me,
For me,
They brighten my pale skin.
Maybe Purple, blue and violet,
Maybe Red, yellow and orange,
Or just black,
You still manage to put life in me.
You tear me,
You crush me,
You destroy me,
But my loyalty to you shall always remain.
The love you have for that next door neighbor,
The hatred you hold for yourself,
The guilt you felt for your sins,
The pride you felt for your good deeds,
The tears you shed for that boy,
I will hold them all,
And never spill.
You may find me peeking out under the couch,
Or in between books,

TO: ME, FROM: ME.

Don't throw me out without a look,
For I may be the one to help you catch your prey with that hook.
Promise me just this,
You will flip through me in a few years, being his,
Adding stories to me as you remember your first Kiss.

14. Purpose

There's something about my purpose, that pulls me deeper into
the state of non-attachment,
And for once I do not fear, the sight I see and the sounds I hear.
As my breathing gets louder,
The air that touches me, I feel,
The slight movement in the corner, I see,
The little shuffle, I hear.
There are days I feel elated,
No more the feeling of being deflated,
Days that I am protected,
To which I am addicted,
Days that I feel sick,
Perhaps because of the thoughts I pick,
Days that I feel tired,
For to exhaust myself was how my brain was wired,
There are days with hysterical crying,
When I'm done trying,
There are days I feel worthy,
When my past memories of insecurities gets cloudy,
Days I am at my best,
Even with all the tests,
Days I am the strongest,

Mostly after a talk with the therapist,
All I can think of during all these times is about my purpose,
where I should be and where I want to be,
But the confusion hasn't cleared.
Till then all I could say is,
Don't know when, but I'll be there,
Don't know how, but I'll get there,
Don't know why, but I wish to be there,
But all along, I won't forget to just be here.

15. Gift of belief

Want something?
Ask for it, believe you have it and in one or the other manner
you will have it,
The world around you, with its destructions, hatred and pain
still remains beautiful,
There still remains salvation, there remains love, there remains
pleasure,
What you desire is always by your side, it's more about whether
you've made the space and if you've made yourself ready for it,
Trust in what's in and around you,
Remember to love what's given and what will be given to you.

16. Sculpture

In the silence amidst the pause,
Her breathes louder than taunting voices,
Strength in her darkness and beauty in her light,
The storm chaotic, her power hypnotic,
She was a muse to look at.

17. Found

She saw the hatred,
read the story behind it.
She saw the breaking,
experienced the healing.
She saw the ruins,
accepted the growth.
She heard the screams of terror,
found the whispers of calmness hidden in them.

18. Softer but stronger

Not so far away was the rim of the well,
Leaped to hold for support, on top was hell,
I will be okay now,
I have to be okay now,
I am okay now,
What a lie.
Clinging on to insecurity,
Self love a mere charity,
Drowning in loneliness,
Depreciation voices so harmonious.
It was time to unlearn,
Perhaps the landing wouldn't be hard again.

19. Cinematic

A Bollywood lover, moments under the rain, for which I'd die,
Burns and scars of acid, painful as I cry,
Your minty breath I craved,
In a stench I remained,
Get rid of everything that ruin you, I preached,
A hypocrite, I leeched on you, demons unleashed,
Around us, cheers of the World Cup resonated,
In between us, screeches of ego elevated,
Blood and pain, a normal,
Healing and peace, something foreign.

20. Blue ticks

Eyes sweating, lips bleeding, cheeks stinging,
I'm okay,
Message sent.
Head spinning, nose running, face red,
I'm okay,
Message delivered.
Body weak, droopy eyes, pained cries,
I'm okay,
Message seen.

21. Still

How it felt to love you,
I would forget all over again,
But I'd still hope to turn all your pain into glory.
How it felt to walk with you,
I would forget and run every time,
But if you fall, I'd still pull you up and teach you to walk again.
How it felt to laugh with you,
I would forget and cry to myself,
But I'd still do anything to see your lips curve up.
Would I come back to you?
Never.
Would I wish the best for you?
Always.

22. Today, tomorrow and everyday

*Today, tomorrow and everyday, let me remember to never live as
if in lack.*

Tell me,

*How can we promise to love ourselves tomorrow when we scream
at ourselves today?*

How do we hope for consistency when we find solace in breaks?

*How do we dream of that big car when the sound of two
wheelers vex us?*

*How do we dream to be in love when that feeling towards
yourself is a mere activity of practice for tomorrow?*

*How do we wish to grow when a minor change becomes the
biggest inconvenience to us?*

*How can we wish to be rich when we look at money with such
poor eyes?*

Caution me,

*Today, tomorrow and everyday, let me remember to never live as
if in lack.*

23. To forget you in reality but keep you in memory

And when breathing gets hard,
I hope your memory is enough to keep me safe.
And when my hands can't hold anything,
I hope the memory of your warmth is enough to stop the shivers.
And when it gets all too hard,
I hope the memory of your smile is enough to make me touch
reality once again.
But who am I kidding?
It won't be easy, it won't feel great, because you cause all that is
uncomfortable.
But believe me when I say, I will find comfort in that chaos as I
realize better that I heal only when I am hurt and with that I
will say I'm done, I will keep you as a lesson but I let you go as a
habit.

24. Communicate

Communicate,

Say it,

Don't hesitate.

You need space?

They won't intrude, they'll leave the place.

You're busy?

They'll come back later, they won't be fussy.

You're tired?

They'll let you rest, that's how they're wired.

You want to be loved?

They won't disappoint, into despair you won't be shoved.

You want to stop?

Be honest, let their smile not drop.

Can't handle?

They have feelings, don't gamble.

Communicate,

Say it.

25. Thank you

Speak,

Greet her hi,

Ask him how,

Call her now,

Let him rant.

Let go,

Cut the I texted first,

Cut the let them text now,

Cut the why do I have to start,

Cut the ego.

Communicate,

Tell her why,

Tell him when,

Tell her where,

Tell him for what.

In a world where everyone is thriving to find the end of the race, if someone has taken the time more than once to acknowledge your existence, sometimes on days you have failed to do so for yourself, don't forget to let them know that they stay appreciated. Tell them, show them.

www.ingramcontent.com/pod-product-compliance
Lightning Source LLC
Chambersburg PA
CBHW020944160726
47993CB00007B/2932